"In *All The Names Given*, the essentia
Knowledge of self, knowledge of others. These poems make
the sublime leap or union of witness to 'with-ness,' so their
knowledge is not speculative but holds together, beautiful
and fraught, the broken burden of honesty: love.
Antrobus is a phenomenal poet."

—ISHION HUTCHINSON, author of *House of Lords and Commons*

"What a beautiful book Raymond Antrobus has written! I love
it. So much pain, so much tenderness, so much music and
invention and passion in *All The Names Given*. Truly, it is terrific.
Antrobus has a special gift of making music from stories and
giving his lyrics gravity and urgency that's inimitable."

—ILYA KAMINSKY, author of *Deaf Republic*

"These poems are revelations. This collection is so obviously
at the forefront of a new canon whose singular and evocative
approach to lyricism and imagistic play demonstrates not only
the necessity of our multilingual and multimodal realities,
but 'the volume of their power,' too."

—MEG DAY, author of *Last Psalm at Sea Level*

"This collection is a brave, tender and generous piece of music,
where family is a cord forever troubled by the process of being
named. With a knife-like precision, *All The Names Given*
manages to caption the speaker's dance with the ghosts of his
bloodline, offering us a haunting study on what we can find
in the silences of history when history is recognized as more
than a noun, when recognized as something alive and kinetic,
something constantly in conversation with the present. I can't
wait to see how this timely book ripples through our world."

—CAMONGHNE FELIX, author of *Build Yourself a Boat*

All The Names Given

Published by Tin House, Portland, Oregon

Distributed by W. W. Norton & Company

Library of Congress Cataloging-in-Publication Data

Names: Antrobus, Raymond, author.
Title: All the names given / Raymond Antrobus.
Description: Portland, Oregon : Tin House, [2021]
Identifiers: LCCN 2021019400 | ISBN 9781951142926 (paperback) |
    ISBN 9781951142933 (ebook)
Subjects: LCGFT: Poetry.
Classification: LCC PR6101.N78 A78 2021 | DDC 821/.92—dc23
LC record available at https://lccn.loc.gov/2021019400

First US Edition 2021
Printed in the USA
Interior design by Jakob Vala

www.tinhouse.com

All The
Names
Given

Raymond
Antrobus

 TIN HOUSE / Portland, Oregon

Contents

*The body as it daydreams goes
towards the earth that belongs to it, from the other earth
that does not.*

—JUAN RAMÓN JIMÉNEZ

Closer Captions

[sound of mouth and arms opening]

Give thanks to the wheels touching tarmac at JFK,
Give thanks to the latches, handles, what we squeeze

into cabins, the wobbling wings, the arrivals,
departures, the long line at the gates, the nerves held,

give thanks to the hand returning the passport, give thanks
to the Lyft driver, the air con, the lightness

of his brown hand at the wheel, the give of rain
on windows asking *where should I live?*

My sister says *stop living in your head.*
Look what that cloud gives. I dream in the back seat

listening to a podcast. The last thing I hear:
Give thanks to your name, Antrobus, to landings

and beginnings, your soul needs time to arrive.

The Acceptance

Dad's house stands again, four years
after being demolished. I walk in.
He lies in bed, licks his rolling paper,
and when I ask *Where have you been?*
We buried you. He says *I know,*

I know. I lean into his smoke, tell him
I went back to Jamaica. *I met your brothers.*
Losing you made me need them. He says
something I don't hear. *What?* Moving lips,
no sound. I shake my head. He frowns.

Disappears. I wake in the hotel room,
heart drumming. I get up slowly, the floor
is wet. I wade into the bathroom,
my father standing by the sink, all the taps
running. He laughs and takes

my hand, squeezes, his ring
digs into my flesh. I open my eyes again.
I'm by a river, a shimmering sheet
of green marble. Red ants crawl up
an oak tree's flaking bark. My hands

are cold mud. I follow the tall grass
by the riverbank, the song, my deaf Orisha
of music, Oshun, in brass bracelets and earrings,
bathes my father in a white dress. I wave. *Hey!*
She keeps singing. The dress turns the river

gold and there's my father surfacing.
He holds a white and green drum. I watch him
climb out the water, drip towards Oshun.
They embrace. My father beats his drum.
With shining hands, she signs: *Welcome.*

Antrobus or Land of Angels

Wherever you are, you touch the bark of trees . . .
different yet familiar.
—CZESŁAW MIŁOSZ

I can be fiendish, I can't be English, say ghosts.
Some with shaved heads, some with cane-rows,
muttering themselves into notebooks.

The barman's eyes in The Antrobus Arms
become sharp gates when I claim to be English.

My mother, born here
My grandfather, the local preacher.

Oh, well then, welcome, he says or *land your angels*.
(There are enigmas in my deafness.)
I stare at the crest of gold lions behind the bar—
I scar the cross of Davidic's line behind the bar—

hear my ghosts say

Fiendish?—

English?

The barman calls the whole village
and my name does the rounds.
My mother drives us to Antrobus Hall.

Two German Shepherds surround
the car. I climb out, it's raining.
The dogs jump, their paws scraping

a new coat of earth on my chest.
A farmer appears, asks if we're descended
from Edmund Antrobus.

Sir Edmund Antrobus, (3rd baronet)
slaver, beloved father
over-seer, owner of plantations

in Jamaica, British Guiana and St Kitts.
I shake my head, avoid the farmer's eye.

*

My mother and I tread the cemetery
of Saint Mark's, Antrobus,
and see everyone buried here is of Antrobus

We look up and see hawks in the ash trees
and sparrows in the wheat fields
and the rain-soaked stones of Antrobus

and after we walk the slick mirrors
of wet roads, the curves
of Barbers Lane, between trees

I take a photo of our shadows, flung
over the red berry bushes

like black coats.

Language Signs

How shall it be known what is spoken? For ye shall speak in the air
  —1 CORINTHIANS 14:8–9

JK Antrobus, grandfather, I dreamt you
returning your reading glasses to your eyes, opening
your bible, pointing at the words you couldn't say.
You pointed at *mercy* and *failure* and then
you pointed at your white hair and your lips and then
at the ceiling of your church as if it were the roof
of your own mouth, and I understood as much as the stone
plaques on the walls or the pews which were wood,
a word that once meant tree.

All the men that raised me are dead, those bastards.
I'm one self-pitying prick of a son. How do I bring
back men who couldn't speak, men lost in books, drinks,
graves? Where do I turn, knowing they left
the hot taps running? I want to say sorry, come to me.
Cut the hedges on your face so I can read your lips.

[sound of connection across time]

On Touch

Touch has a memory. O say, Love, say,
What can I do to kill it and be free
In my old liberty?
　　　—JOHN KEATS

Salute the touches of teachers,
dentists and therapists who untangle us

from their chairs. Salute bin men
recyclers, carpenters, plumbers and barbers.

Remember the way of moving
that says your back has been rubbed, your neck

brushed, your front doors cleared, your shelves
stocked. Now you have nothing

but long sides and hedges and a sudden memory
of your first teacher-crush, Miss Walker

touching your curls, saying she liked it like that
soft, short on the sides. You wanted

the world in that shape forever. For years
you always got the same trim from the same barber

which became its own intimacy.
You rub your hands over your own spiky head,

remember your barber, ready to gown you,
fold your ears back and run razors around your sides

so someone you want would touch you later.

Her Taste

Funny that my mother was a clown
a college dropout who joined the circus
with another clown who made inflatable giants.
It's funny. His name was George,
a Marxist who swore he was serious

when he said the men who tried
to mow him down in a car one night
were sent by Thatcher, so he fled England
to hide while my mother pulled another
man at a Ska and Reggae night in Hackney

who was tall and afro'ed and swooned
her under the music.
I'm Seymour, he said, pointing
at his eyes, saying *the more I see
the more I see*, and she burped.

George (who was serious when he said
he didn't want children) came back
to England to find my mother
pregnant and he struck her in the face
but ended up staying in the same house

saying he'd help raise the child,
but wasn't serious, he left
and my mother and Seymour,
(who was my father), raised my sister and me.
Thirty years later my mother says she's

holding her head higher at seventy.
She never needed a man.
Of course I wonder where her taste
came from. Her own father was quiet,
detached and serious all his life,
reaching out his arms for God
while his children crawled at his feet.

Text and Image

Tabitha: *y haven't u told me u luv me*
Raymond: *I'm literally writing you love poems*

you're trying to send me a portrait
of a lady on fire but the link won't load

so I don't know what it shows
and you're in the cinema rustling

in the dark and we think we aren't
doing things the old way, our marriage

is new age, no more you complete me crap,
have your own life and I have my life

and it's tricky and easy while we're doing
long distance but how can I show you

my love is unfolding if my words
can't reach you glowing and wild?

DEATH OF SIR E. ANTROBUS (4th Baronet) OWNER AND GUARDIAN OF STONEHENGE

Headline from The Times, *May 15th 1915*

And there's my English grandmother,
Barbara Antrobus by the fire,

TV on and her dog, Coco,
huddled on her lap.

You know, the Antrobuses
owned Stonehenge, she says

as sure as if her own hand
rested on the stone.

The Antrobuses refused
millions of pounds

to sell it to America.
That's our history,

keeping those stones
where they were found.

Her story made the fire
relight itself.

Flare light
on my grandmother,

a minister's wife,
who prided herself

only as God's servant.
At Christmas she watched

the Queen's speech
hands on her lap

thinking face
quiet as a private fence.

When she died no giant
monuments were passed

our way. But she sat up
in her hospital bed

and said *the children
are by the lake,*

don't let them fall in
and it's astonishing

how clearly I can hear her
and those children now,

how lasting their voices
inside us. How deeply known.

[sound of time passing]

[music of urgent kindness]

[ripens quietly]

My Mother Skimming Her Scrapbook

This is me, sitting on the bed next to a stack of books, a reading light

This is me driving a red mini metro through a red light

Me, going for a walk with an old boyfriend

Me, rolling a spliff on somebody's balcony

This is my girlhood with the dog that was run over

Me, dropping out of English Lit class but keeping the reading list

Me in church reading Bertrand Russell's 'Why I'm Not A Christian'

Me, noticing my father isn't happy

Me, with cigarette ash on my skirt

Me, as the little sister at the table with both my brothers

*There's my Mum, telling us again about the plane that machine gunned
the house and her fall down the stairs that killed her first child*

Me, looking ghostly

Me, leaving the house, probably forgetting my keys

Every Black Man

in my grandmother's mind was Desmond Tutu. She wrote
his words in journals and kept them by her husband's
sermons but when she met my dark dreadlocked Jamaican father

he was drunk and he didn't like the way she looked at him
and some shouting started and he hit my pregnant mother
and my grandmother shouted *You black devil!* But

this story starts differently depending on who I ask, maybe
with an English missionary to the *dark continent,*
or maybe with my father's first drink when he was eleven

and a teenage girl gave him the bottle and took him
into the bush and said to drink it, pulled down his pants
and made him fuck. Maybe with the Highland Clearances,

the poverty of farmers that lived by birch trees
and set to the seas with all the winds that whipped their sails
and put everything behind my father's family name,

Birch, maybe with the dark roots of money and the cities that grew
from phallus and father doing holy work
or maybe with someone else's father raising his hand

to someone else's mother or maybe when someone's mother
forgives someone's father, maybe my father had no memory
of any incident where he wasn't a victim,

he said my grandmother actually called him *nigger*
but telling Tabitha this story while sitting by the Mississippi,
she says, *That's some nigga shit!* and I laugh but I never saw
my father and my grandmother in the same room my whole life.

[sound of self divided]

[running]

[breath on paper]

Plantation Paint

After Lorna Goodison and A Plantation Burial *in The Historic New Orleans Collection, 1860 oil on canvas by John Antrobus*

Tabitha the art conservator,
squints at the colour,
tells me the paint

depicting the black
of these men
huddled for a burial

will decay before
the cypress trees
surrounding them

will decay.
There are several kinds
of black, she says and

the cypress trees
surrounding them is all I see
as we stand, alive

in this otherwise
empty gallery.
Why am I like this?

What am I like?
Who does
it matter to?

All details question
my way
of seeing.

I worry
what kind of black
would mark me?

I am not the paint
made from vine twigs
or burnt shells.

I am not the lamp full of oil.
Tabitha, tell me
how you'd paint me?

Tell me if I'm closer
to the white painter
with my name than I am

to the black preacher,
his hands wide to the sky,
the mahogany rot

of heaven. Sorry,
but you know by now
that I can't mention trees

without every shade
of my family
appearing and disappearing.

Heartless Humour Blues

My mother says my father had a heartless sense of humour.
That winter she fell, ice on the road—

She can't forget her bruise, his laughter.
Not even his shadow helped her up or soothed her.

He watched from the kerb—boozy red-eyed Dad—
laughed when she said *he had a heartless sense of humour.*

I think that's how he handled pain, drink his only tutor.
Maybe laughter was the only thing he had?

No, my mother says, *he had a heartless sense of humour.*
In Hackney Downs, his past became my future,

walking drunk by filter beds, noticing how grass sags,
laughing at myself with my heartless sense of humour.

He'd tell some tragic story, then laugh, his jaw looser,
and if laughter won a round of drinks, be glad

of what can be bought with that heartless sense of humour.
My mother tried again and the next man abused her—

another man with a drink and cigarettes to drag,
laughed with my father's heartless sense of humour.

When Tabitha said our cousin stabbed his father
I laughed, and she closed up, turned away, sour.

Ray, where did you get that heartless sense of humour?

A Short Speech Written On Receipts

Are we about to enter history or
Café Tout de Suite on Verret Street?
The waitress has a face as much African
as Vietnamese, as if even the grease
on her white shirt came from
a long line of proud Creole cooks.
I have always felt guilty needing any
small service. My mother is a market
trader. As a child I once kicked
a woman who kept talking without buying.
I'm thinking my mother could do everything
right and still not survive. I've not grown out
of carrying anxious bags into every room
where I become a customer. It's a thing
if I'm passing a market and the street hagglers
want me to name a price. It's hard to say
what that should be when I see my mother
in tired light saying this was a good day, this
was a bad day. This waitress has a bandana
tied tight around her head, apron around
her waist—all her kitchen sweats look
listened to. Sometimes I feel guilty asking
someone to repeat, but she repeats and
nobody dies. Maybe kindness is how
you take down the stalls. This waitress
and my mother would show up at my funeral,

a short speech written on receipts.
They'd stand next to my coffin, say
we made this hungry man's dish,
slow cooked his fish and he ate, messy
and grateful as he lived.

It Was Cold Under My Breath

Mum, I knew you heard
the day I called you *bitch*
under my breath as I sat
by the fan heater, drying

from a bath and you told me
to turn it off. It was cold.
What? you said, holding
the leash on yourself,

giving me the chance
to make another world
where hard words don't fly
from a boy

What? I knew my father
would've belted me right there,
but you were alone,
too tired to turn.

You said *I don't think
I heard anything* and left the room,
and I hated you for not
belting the brat out of me

[sound of mirrors breaking inside mirrors]

On Vanity

I pass 'Ray's Glass and Frames' on my way to the gym.
All of me appears in the shop's mirror, all my years

of pouting, still with me—that tight
and vain language of my face.

Becky once broke the silence on the train:
You look better in photographs. At home, I looked

in the mirror and took a photo of myself
taking a photo of myself and kept no photo

of myself smiling. I don't love my body.
I don't think I'm beautiful. My body is an object

and all the names it is given. I'm grateful
my mother never called me beautiful. Perhaps

she said it to a photograph of my face,
perhaps she held it up and kissed what she named.

Text and Image

Raymond: *in the dream I was in a packed cinema.*
I had a remote for the screen, I flick channels,

turn on captions and no one seemed to mind.
Some forgotten Macaulay Culkin film came on

and laughter erupted, then a film trailer started.
I'm on screen talking to the camera but what I'm saying

isn't subtitled. Behind me, a man in a hood
wearing a strange shiny blue tracksuit, he takes off

his hood and it's Macaulay Culkin! He's looking around
and sees me looking at him and quickly puts his hood back on.

A woman with a wide chin is sitting next to me making hmm noises.
On screen, I'm peering up a faintly lit staircase and all goes grainy.

I see that the tattoos on my arm are just scribbled pen marks
then the wide chin woman, realising it's me on the screen, says

you know, you really missed an opportunity,
you're talking about your mother

but you're not really talking about your mother
and I turn to see my mother's face flickering in and out of light.

[sound of broken beginning]

On Desperation

She left you months ago / when you see her
on a train platform / you talk and talk
to keep her there / in front of you /

the last mirror in the world / the train she needs
goes by / she stands like a book
that doesn't want your eye / she says

she's going to meet someone / pries herself away
from your itchy steam / you say ok / you know
later someone will become her new love /

you'll dream of her fucking / all night in her new
and perfect house / you don't own
a house but there you'll be / watching

your 2am text / lit / like a dog panting
on her screen / hot rattling engine / pile
of oily pity / sticky bathroom / lonely grease /

air no one wants to suck /

And That

After seeing a childhood friend outside a chicken shop in Dalston

Chicken wings / and dat
Boss man / salt in them / and dat

Don't assault man / give man a nap—
Kin / Big man / no steroid / and dat

Dark times / new street lights / and dat
How's man? / I'm getting by / and dat

Still / boy dem / harass
Not beefin' / Not tagged / man / still trapped

Cycle man / pedallin' / and dat
On road / new pavements / levelled / and dat

Crackney changed / still / stay dwelling / and dat
Paradise moves / but I got to land grab

We E8 / East man / ain't got to adapt
Our Kingdom / got no land to hand back

Man / chat breeze / chat
Trade winds / and dat

You out ends / got good job / legit / and dat?
Locked off man dem / stay plotting / and dat

Rah, Ray / Flower shorts? / You hipster / in dat
Man gone / Vegan? / No chicken wings / and dat

Maybe It Was Our Dark

After Frank O'Hara

From the passenger seat I point
my camera towards the passing hills.

A truck driver deliberately obscures the view
and because of his game of getting in my way

I miss a good photo and am instead left with his
satisfied laughter driving away.

Is this why I'm not a photographer?
You can be more than one thing at once

I said with my mother's eyes
and my dead father's habit

of stroking the patch
of hair below his lip.

My cousin keeps
posting army knives

on the internet for the LOLs.
He lives in the mountains

and would drive a truck
if he could afford it.

For Cousin John

. . . land of shades!
—WILLIAM BLAKE

Your voice, a red and white flag,
a teatime tablecloth. *Slavery*

happened long ago, it means
nothing now. I prepare silence,

practise each time for a calm dinner

but you lift a fork, unsettle the territory.

I can't stop seeing the child
pulled from a home of hissing

and raised by our grandmother
who was endlessly scraping plates

between us. With her gone

something shifts at our table and you

keep sharpening the somewhere else
in me. No, I don't know what it's like

to live in a small military town
or how you fit where everyone is white.

Do you hold up England

by its gilt edges, best china handles?

What secretly stirs your tea? *Cousin,*
we all alone in these streets. I wish you

horses in rain and fields of broken gates.
I wish you a surprise party of sober mothers

holding a Thomas the Tank Engine birthday cake.
I wish you glistening grapes and radiated rooms.

When we stood shoulder to shoulder
at our grandmother's funeral I didn't hear you cry

but I felt your quivering, saw your red face,
the fallen flags in your eyes, Cousin, why couldn't you

let us see what you were burying? Cousin

I wish sunlight on all your fields

What does sound mean to us?

—CHRISTINE SUN KIM

. . . books on peace were printed in the midst of disorder,
and books on silence in the midst of noise.

—JUAN RAMÓN JIMÉNEZ

The Royal Opera House (with Stage Captions)

A play. An all black cast in a South African township: we see them sing their songs and play their instruments. We follow a boy through the townships, we see his mother killed by rebel soldiers, a new shore of blood pools the floor, the boy sleeps next to her corpse.

[sound of speechless poverty]

We see the boy saved by his uncle who also ends up shot trying to protect the boy, we see the boy find his cousin (a woman) who does things on her own and helps the boy reluctantly, we see her shot too.

[sound of blood in the air]

We see the boy grow up on the streets and learn all the languages and have him become a hustler, a man about town, we see him marry a woman who only wants him for money. We don't see where the woman comes from or what she is escaping or what she could be a prisoner of.

[sound of newer emptiness]

We see the boy marry the woman because he's all flash and hustle, we see he works hard and dreams harder, we see the boy cross borders, trying to get to this gloss, *just one speck, one atom on the glazed surface we call America.*

[sound of mirror refusing reflection]

We're asked to have more compassion for the man who makes it out alive than anyone poverty trapped, we see his best friend stabbed to death in a robbery, we see the boy huddle over his friend's corpse.

[sound of English sharpening]

We don't see the oil or the Coca-Cola Company or land rights or coups or the arms industry or the drug companies. We don't see who owns the ships, who owns the land, who owns the business, who owns the road. We don't muddy ourselves with details that complicate, we don't see whose body is left in the desert, or a city street or an ocean. We see men on the stage become criminal by yanking hoods over their heads.

[American music]

We see them hide their face, we see them keep a gun or a knife in their pocket or a gold tooth in their gums. We see all the black bodies in this play hide the white man who wrote it.

[sound of the future working]

The writer, educated at Rhodes and Oxford University, has somehow freed himself from his own history. We hear a line in the play that has the boy, older now, say, just before entering the American border, *I will write my own story*

[unstoppable singing]

and this is where everyone in the Royal Opera House, Black, white, whatever, rises to their feet and shouts and hollers and claps and cries and none of the silences, none of them are filled.

Horror Scene as Black English Royal (Captioned)

One night, in the shower, you look at your hands and they are your
great-great-great-Grandfather's owner's hands. They are leaning on the
walls of his boiling house

[sound of camp fires]

Your feet are the whitest sugar and you don't know where to step or
what you're really holding when you sneak into your Grandmother's
bedroom, her jewels hanging by the mirror

[sound of secret room]

Is all of this what your great-great-great-Grandfather would have thrown
you overboard for? Does it matter? Does your blood have to make all this
old centurion noise?

[sound of fractures]

You won't strain to hear who or what is at the bottom of the ocean.
What ship will turn, sink, rot, burn your mouth when you speak your
reparation receipts?

[sound of sinking]

Your tongue tasting the iron bit, the River Nile, the Gulf Coast, the
Thames, the Abeng horn. When you cry, what rhythm, the crown?
What is this sound, erupting from the whitest black blood in the land?

The Rebellious

hold what they can
in front of a supermarket

or police station
or voting booths. I am

kind to the man
sitting next to me

in C.L.R. James Library, even if
his breathing disturbs me.

Can we graciously disagree?
I am tired of people

not knowing the volume
of their power. Who doesn't

deserve
some silence at night?

[sound of someone wanting my skin]

Claude McKay

It must be tragic for a sensitive Negro to be a poet.
Why didn't you choose pugilism instead of poetry for a profession?
—GEORGE BERNARD SHAW

Let me keep my fists
in my pocket, fidget
my ink, let me stumble

to my corner, take my stall,
see who squeezes
my back, grips my face.

Look, the floor.
Is that my blood?
My tooth? My island?

At Every Edge

One inmate squeezed my hand like a letter
he'd been hoping for. In the workshop,
he read his poem. I applauded.
He hugged me. He smelt of stale soap.
Leaning in, his stubble sandpapered
my softer jaw. He tells me what he did,
says he was drunk the night he blacked out,
opened his eyes in the kitchen, his wife
who wanted divorce, on the floor,
dead. I see his wedding ring. I wish
I knew her name so I could plant it here.

A Paper Shrine

When the ten year old boy reads
a poem for his dead granddad
I push back tears. *Don't want*
to spoil him with too much notice
from the professional poet
his teacher says, making me
a boy again, staring at his shoes.

Later the boy asks *if writing*
is emotional and I notice myself
telling him how once in a café
I watched a man, chunks of his arm
lost to needles, as he tried
to make a tiny house with the leaflets
left on the windowsill.

[talking in sleep]

Upwards (For Ty Chijioke)

After Christopher Gilbert

The last place the sun reaches in my garden
is the back wall where the ivy
grows above the stinging nettles.

What are they singing to us?
Is it painless to listen?
Will music soothe our anxious house?

Speech falls on things like rain
sun shades all the feelings of having a heart.
Here, take my pulse, take my breath,

take my arms as I drift off

Text and Image

Tabitha: *Dreamt I was in my studio,*
conserving this painting, slowly sharpening scalpels.

I'm neat and focused until my fingernails
became a large feeling that the painting couldn't understand me.

Meanwhile my fingernails start scratching the canvas,
I lose it and hold the painting, tearing the whole thing in half.

Then there are twelve more paintings at my feet
(Warhol's, Marclay's, Hockney's) and I'm picking up each

and tearing and tearing until my finger nails fell off, became swords
and all the paintings became my uncle (who was murdered)

but there was no blood on his body, just bright blue
and yellow paint and someone kept saying

master, master, master, master, master.

Captions & A Dream For John T. Williams of the Nuu-chah-nulth tribe

                                        [sound of unstable air]

He fell facing away from the police officer,
four bullet holes on the left side of his body,
hands holding a block of cedar wood
and a three-inch blade he used to carve
canoes and faces into totem poles.

                              [announcing it is not over]

The police officer said:
I yelled at him to drop the knife.

                                  [sound of something left out]

It took five seconds to shoot.

John T. Williams' brother sat
on the pavement. He didn't turn away
from the block of cedar wood
that still shone on the road.

                                        [careful speech]

The reporters pushed microphones
into his face. *My brother was deaf*

[sound of no season]

He spoke each word
for the trembling broadcast as if
his brother could still read his lips.

[sound stolen]

They took something beautiful from us

[wailing]

I dream of the crosswalk
at Boren Avenue and Howell Street.
In my dream John T. Williams
appears in a whaling canoe. When
he paddles, the water doesn't ripple.

I ask if he has a favourite sound. The lake
melts, becomes a narrow street. A kettle
boils silently on the pavement.
John T. Williams points at a house.
There are still keys hanging

in the green door. I follow him
into the living room.
He is setting the table for a meal.
I ask nothing. He pours tea.
There is tapping at the window.

Someone is humming in the garden
by a totem pole, summoning
the sound of hands
leaving
a mark.

[   ]

[   ]

For Tyrone Givans

The paper said *putting him in jail*
without his hearing aids was like
putting him in a hole in the ground.

There are no hymns
for deaf boys. But who can tell
we're deaf without speaking to us?

Tyrone's name was misspelled
in the HMP Pentonville prison system.
Once, I was handcuffed,

shoved into a police van. I didn't hear
the officer say why. I was saved
by my friend's mother who threw herself

in the road and refused to let the van drive away.
Who could have saved Tyrone?
James Baldwin attempted suicide

after each of his loves
jumped from bridges or overdosed.
He killed his characters, made them

kill themselves—*Rufus, Richard,*
Black men who couldn't live like this.
Tyrone, I won writing awards

bought new hearing aids and heard
my name through the walls.
I bought a signed Baldwin book.

The man who sold it to me didn't know
you, me or Baldwin.
I feel I rescued it. I feel failed.

Tyrone, the last time I saw you alive
I'd dropped my pen
on the staircase

didn't hear it fall but you saw and ran
down to get it, handed it to me
before disappearing, said,

you might need this.

I Ran Away from Home to See How Long It'd Take My Mother to Notice

Are you my drunk teacher who took our game of rounders way too seriously? Are you the boy who said I had the ugliest smile on the playground? Are you the girl who toe punted my balls and made me a piss sack of blood? the girlfriend who slept with women behind my back, said it wasn't cheating? I don't know what I'm saying, would you be my friend? I spent hours in the house alone as a child, I left fingerprints on my sister's CDs so the music kept skipping! I wanted her friends to be my friends but I wasn't invited to her parties. Are you the party? Are you my Dad lying on the sofa, saying *I'll soon be dead?* When I pull 'What Is Existentialism?' off my mother's shelf Simone de Beauvoir says *The movement of my transcendence appears futile*, I don't know what that means so I put it back, fuck! Who loves me? I'm testing everyone! I need space for all my old and new gooey needs and projections, I need constant blaring validation alarms, give me award ceremonies, please observe my wall of fame: Best Second-Guessing Over-Achiever, Best Internal Monologue While Drying Dishes, Best Self-Promoter at the Charity Fundraiser, Best Awkward Silence in a Moving Vehicle, Best Bad Advice to a Couple in Crisis, Best Non-Smoker in the Smoking Area, Most Self-Centred Fear during the Global Pandemic, Lifetime Achievement Award For Most Convincing Head Nod In A Crowded Pub, Most Triggered Person In An Empty House

Bredrin

I was twelve / you were sixteen / boy-friendin' my older sister / Bredrin,
my music Roots Manueva'ed you / *this is sick, Bredrin!*

You taught me to rev road / I crashed / your Moped ended.
You dusted me down / *what's the damage mi Bredrin?*

An older boy at school missiled his shoe at me / Bredrin
you front-lined the gate / despite your foot in a cast / *test him!*

Boy'ed him up by his hood / *to rass, don't fuck wit' mi Bredrin.*
Then Mr. Drinkwater thought you called him a *bread bin.*

When your three year old son swore at me / I got vex. No blessin' /
You said *nuh tell me how to raise mi yout / you're in my yard / Bredrin*

Years later / the water still bitter / I summon Braithwaite /
time / is short / and life / is short / and breath / is short / Bredrin.

Sutton Road Cemetery

After Eavan Boland

His mother had driven him back to London in the half light,
He sighed in the passenger seat. They stopped
by the Southend seas as the wind picked up and
clouds thinned into English women. All the stones
had said nothing of their names as he skimmed them wide
across the waves.

Earlier, when he'd found the grave of his great-grandmother
by the elderberry tree it was the one time he'd wanted
someone white to appear and ask
where he was from. It would've been no skin off him
to point at her stone and say

here

In Law

I feel the cuffs in his voice when he greets me.
It should go without saying that you are no man's property,

that I would not touch you anywhere you don't want.
These things have nothing to do with bullets

even though I'm never far from the father
that would kill me faster than life can flash

blue then darkness, so let me say, *love*,
my arms are in the air.

Arose

My father called my mother *Rose* for short.
Once I asked him how it ever worked out
between them. *The sex* he smirked, *the sex
was that good.* I was twelve, and betrayed. But
I'd seen him in my mother's garden that
summer, growing sunflowers. I'd seen him
paint all the walls in her house and my mother
chose the colour. I'd seen him bend by
my mother's bicycle, mend her tires, rock
his head to a record she was playing and ask her
if he could borrow it. I'd seen the way
he walked down the street grinning with
new music. Once I'd seen him stand behind
my mother's market stall when a woman held
up a necklace my mother made, and ask him
how much it was, and he turned to my mother,
said *Rose?* And he said it like something in him
grew towards the light.

On Being A Son

my mother
      asking how
to open a tab
on her laptop,
      to email a photo,
calling to ask—
can you change
      the lightbulb
at the top of the stairs?
my mother
      spending hours
helping me find
      a doctor's form,
a hearing aid battery,
      any misplaced thing,
my mother
who keeps leaving
      her keys in the doors
or on the walls,
      who keeps saying
I might have to change
      the locks, mother
of self-sufficiency,
      of beads and trolleys,
of handlebars,
      short-tempered mother

of resistance
  of pliers and thread
of liquorice and seaweed
  on the table,
lonely mother,
mother needs-no-man,
  mother deserves my cooking,
deserves a long sleep,
  a cuppa, a garden
of lavender mothers,
all her heads up,
  mother's tooth
falls out, mother
  dyes her hair,
don't say greying
  say sea salt
and cream.

Outside the marriage registry in Jefferson Parish there's a 10-foot statue of Thomas Jefferson

I felt-tip the forms
declaring *alien immigrant.*
Where the form asks my race,

I write Black / White,
hand it to a man
who points at my words,

says I cannot be two races.
His short wool hair flinches
in the air-conditioned room;

his badge says his name is Jeff.

Article III

Name
Eston Hemings

Mother
Sally Hemings

Father
Thomas Jefferson

Race
Black / White

Ruler of My Heart by Irma Thomas is the first song on our wedding playlist

Tabitha and I are newlyweds.
We lunge across the field
towards the Mississippi.

Two fishes
from different rivers.
We hear the keys, horns

of 'Ruler of My Heart,'
We take hands,
We dance, we dance

My heart.
Driver of my soul
Where can you be?

A riverboat glosses the shore,
Tabitha and I are newlyweds.

we water
    we steam
        we shake

[sound of strangers arriving]

[squirming in suit]

[sound of light between us]

Loveable

The first time you told me you loved me
I didn't say it back,

which is to say
that I was not loveable.

Those who have loved me before say
I made them feel second to some dream I was having.

You know the thing with dreams
you're the only one that sees them

so when I say I didn't know what was talking
the first night you said you loved me I mean

I needed to hear it in the morning
hear it said when neither of us

could be anyone
except who we are

Closer Captions

After Christine Sun Kim

[muffled]

[sound of one story]

[heart accelerating]

[sound of skin covering bodies]

[sound of wider seeing]

I lose my hearing aids
and move more fluid

the same way I do
when I swim the way
I do when I sex

the thing
the neighbours hear

through the walls
is me being pushed
out of myself

It's silence that stills
the noise in my eyes.

Reader, this is the place
I try to take you
when I close them.

Notes on the Poems

The epigraph from Juan Ramón Jiménez is extracted from Robert Bly's translation of the poem 'Night Piece' that appears in *Lorca & Jiménez: Selected Poems* (1997, Beacon Press).

Antrobus (my English mother's name) is a locational surname from the place in Cheshire, England, called Antrobus. Anyone with the 'Antrobus' name can be linked to this village. It interests me that 'Antrobus' is often assumed to be foreign to English, when in fact the name is so anciently English (Norse) that it has become foreign to itself.

The Sound Of / Closer Captions are visual art exhibitions by Deaf sound artist Christine Sun Kim that inspired the use of captions in the book. Sun Kim rewrites captioned text from films in order to revise the listening experience from hearing centric to Deaf centric. When thinking about captions and subtitles, Sun Kim asks, 'Does sound itself have to be a sound? Could it be a feeling, emotion or an object? Could time itself become a sound?' Some of the captions that appear in this book are lifted from Christine Sun Kim's work and some are my own.

I created a radio programme titled 'Inventions In Sound' with Eleanor McDowall produced by Falling Tree Productions as a companion to this book. The show was aired on BBC Radio 4 in March 2021. You can access the show on BBC Sounds. There is also a visual version and transcript version available.

'The Acceptance': This poem would not exist without Chris Abani, and the poet Arielle John, who had shared with me a version of the Orisha myth in which Oshun has 'one large ear and one small ear' and appears as 'the deaf goddess of music'.

'Antrobus or Land of Angels': '*Wherever you are, you touch the bark of trees . . . different yet familiar*' is a Czesław Miłosz line taken from his poem 'Throughout Our Lands' (1961) trans. Robert Hass.

Information on Sir Edmund Antrobus was found at Legacy of British-Slave Ownership Database at UCL—https://www.ucl.ac.uk/lbs/person/view/23866

'*Touch has a memory. O say, love, say. / What can I do to kill it and be free / In my old liberty?*'—is from John Keats' poem 'To—(what can I do to drive away)', from *Keats: Poems Published in 1820* (2017, Pinnacle).

'Every Black Man' has the line 'from phallus and father doing holy work' and is lifted from Adrienne Rich's book of poems *the school among the ruins: poems 2000–2004* (2006, W. W. Norton).

'For Cousin John': '. . . *land of shades!*' is a William Blake line from *The Complete Poetry & Prose of William Blake* (2008, University of California Press). I remember hearing a story that William Blake was often seen shouting lines of poems at trees and this was a line that was once heard.

'*Cousin, we all alone in these streets*' is based on a lyric by the rapper Prodigy from the Mobb Deep song 'Shook Ones, Pt. II'.

'Plantation Paint' is in conversation with the poem 'To Make Various Sorts of Black' by Lorna Goodison from *Supplying Salt and Light* (2013, McClelland & Stewart) and the painting *A Plantation Burial* by John Antrobus (1860, oil on canvas).

'Maybe It Was Our Dark' is in conversation with Frank O'Hara's poem 'Why I'm Not A Painter' (2008, Knopf).

'Royal Opera House' was commissioned by Christine Sun Kim and Niels Van Tomme for the 'Activating Captions' exhibition at ARGOS in Brussels. This poem is a revision of the play 'A Man Of Good Hope' written by Jonny Steinberg.

'. . . just one speck . . . on the glazed surface we call America' is a line by Adrienne Rich from her book *the school among the ruins*.

'Horror Scene as Black English Royal' was written in 2019 after seeing the headline 'How Black Will The Royal Baby Be' on CNN. I happened to be in the audiology clinic at the time I saw the headline on TV (which was on mute with the captions on).

'The Rebellious' is dedicated to Rashan Charles.

'Claude McKay': After George Bernard Shaw met Claude McKay and said, 'It must be tragic for a sensitive Negro to be a poet. Why didn't you choose pugilism instead of poetry for a profession?,' this anecdote appears in Claude McKay's remarkable autobiography *A Long Way From Home* (1937, L. Furman).

'Upwards (For Ty Chijioke)': *Speech falls on things like rain* is a line by Christopher Gilbert taken from his book *Across The Mutual Landscape* (1984, Graywolf).

'Bredrin': *time / is short / and life / is short / and breath / is short* is a line from Kamau Brathwaite's book of poems *Other Exiles* (1975, Oxford University Press).

'Captions & A Dream For John T Williams of the Nuu-chah-nulth tribe': The details of this case were gathered from 'The Ruderman White Paper on Media Coverage of Law Enforcement Use of Force and Disability', a fascinating and distressing academic paper by David M. Perry PhD and Lawrence Carter-Long that highlights some crucial gaps in police and media training in handling disabled members of the public. The conclusion to the study is that violence against people with disabilities has been rising steeply for the past decade and victims continue to be blamed in the media for their own deaths with little to zero police and societal accountability.

'For Tyrone Givans' was commissioned by Simon Armitage and Jude Kelly for the 'Ripples of Hope' project in response to article 5 of the Universal Declaration of Human Rights—*No one shall be subjected to torture or to cruel, inhuman or degrading treatment or punishment*. 'Putting him in prison without his hearing aids was like putting him in a hole in the ground' is a headline from a 22 Jan 2020 article in *The Guardian*—https://www.theguardian.com /society/2020/jan/22/prison-death-tyrone-givans-deaf-hmp-pentonville. I give thanks to Tyrone's family, our teachers at Blanche Nevile Deaf School and Abdul Ali.

'Sutton Road Cemetery' is inspired by Eavan Boland's beautiful book of poems, *Against Love Poetry* (2003, Norton).

Acknowledgements

Many thanks to the editors of the following publications where poems from this book first appeared, often in older versions: *POETRY*, *Poetry Review*, Poets.org, *Prairie Schooner*, The Adroit Journal, *New Humanist*, *The Rumpus*, Split This Rock, Zoeglossia and *More Fiya: An Anthology of Black British Poetry*, ed. Kayo Chingonyi (Canongate, 2022).

Thanks to the poets and artists who inspired, engaged and encouraged me through the writing of *All The Names Given*, particularly Chris Abani, Phoebe Boswell, Christine Sun Kim, Ilya Kaminsky, Mimi Khalvati, Don Paterson, Shira Erlichman, Jay Bernard, R.A. Villanueva, Jeffrey Mansfield, Caleb Azumah Nelson, Guy Gunaratne, Othello De'Souza-Hartley, Pádraig Ó Tuama, Will Harris, Matthew Siegel, Jack Underwood, Nick Makoha, Keith Jarrett, Hanif Abdurraqib, Victoria Adukwei Bulley, Gboyega Odubanjo, Belinda Zhawi, Arielle John, Karisma Price, Taylor Johnson, Marwa Helal, Hala Alyan, Meg Day, Hannah Lowe, Roger Robinson, Dante Micheaux, Rachel Long, Jillian Weise, Inua Ellams, Toni Stuart, Vahni Capildeo, Wayne Holloway-Smith, Anthony Anaxagorou, Malika Booker, Margaret Busby, Bernardine Evaristo, Peter Kahn and Nathalie Teitler.

Thanks Picador and Tin House team, especially Kishani Widyaratna, Salma Begum, Elizabeth DeMeo and Niki Chang.

Shout out to the poets and teachers associated with the Complete Works, Cave Canem, Obsidian Foundation and Speaking Volumes.

In loving memory of Ty, Mr. Emmerson, Tyrone Givans, Jules Baker, Michael Horovitz, Jean 'Binta' Breeze and my grandfather J. K. Antrobus and grandmother Barbara Antrobus.

Mum, you asked when I was going to write you a book. Here's your book. I love you, thank you.

Further Reading

Diary Of A Newlywed Poet (*Diario de un poeta reciencasado*)
Juan Ramón Jiménez

Other Exiles
Kamau Brathwaite

Into Each Room We Enter without Knowing
Charif Shanahan

Supplying Salt and Light
Lorna Goodison

Across the Mutual Landscape
Christopher Gilbert

Ordinary Beast
Nicole Sealey

Hot Earth Cold Earth
James Berry

Mute
Raymond Luczak